Christmas Carols Songbook

Table of Contents

Jingle Bells

Dashing through the snow
In a one-horse open sleigh
O'er the fields we go
Laughing all the way
Bells on bob tail ring
Making spirits bright
What fun it is to ride and
sing
A sleighing song tonight!
Jingle bells, jingle bells
Jingle all the way
Oh, what fun it is to ride
In a one-horse open sleigh,
hey! Jingle bells, jingle bells
Jingle all the way
Oh, what fun it is to ride
In a one-horse open sleigh!
A day or two ago, I thought
I'd take a ride And soon,
Miss Fanny Bright

Was seated by my side
The horse was lean and lank
Misfortune seemed his lot
He got into a drifted bank
And then we got upsot
Jingle bells, jingle bells
Jingle all the way
Oh, what fun it is to ride
In a one-horse open sleigh, hey!

Jingle bells, jingle bells
Jingle all the way
Oh, what fun it is to ride
In a one-horse open sleigh!
A day or two ago
The story I must tell
I went out on the snow
And on my back I fell
A gent was riding by
In a one-horse open sleigh
He laughed as there I sprawling
lie

But quickly drove away
Jingle bells, jingle bells
Jingle all the way
Oh, what fun it is to ride In
a one-horse open sleigh,
hey!
Jingle bells, jingle bells
Jingle all the way
Oh, what fun it is to ride
In a one-horse open sleigh!
Now the ground is white
Go it while you're young
Take the girls tonight
And sing this sleighing song
Just get a bobtailed bay
Two forty as his speed
Hitch him to an open sleigh

And crack! You'll take the
lead
Jingle bells, jingle bells
Jingle all the way
Oh, what fun it is to ride

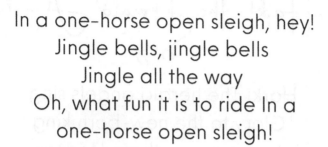

In a one-horse open sleigh, hey!
Jingle bells, jingle bells
Jingle all the way
Oh, what fun it is to ride In a
one-horse open sleigh!

Hark! The Herald Angels Sing

Hark! The herald angels sing
"Glory to the new-born king
Peace on earth and mercy
mild
God and sinners reconciled"
Joyful all ye nations rise
Join the triumph of the skies
With angelic host proclaim
"Christ is born in Bethlehem"

Hark! The herald angels sing
"Glory to the new-born king"
Hail the heaven-born Prince
of Peace!
Hail the Sun of Righteousness!
Light and life to all
He brings
Risen with healing in His
wings

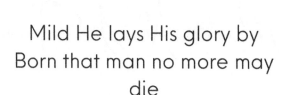

Mild He lays His glory by
Born that man no more may
die

Born to raise the sons of
earth
Born to give them second
birth
Hark! The herald angels sing
"Glory to the new-born king"
Hark! The herald angels sing
"Glory to the new-born king
Peace on earth and mercy
mild
God and sinners reconciled"
Joyful all ye nations rise
Join the triumph of the skies
With angelic host proclaim
"Christ is born in Bethlehem"
Hark! The herald angels sing
"Glory to the new-born king"
"Glory to the new-born king"

O Come All Ye Faithful

O Come all ye faithful
Joyful and triumphant
O come ye, O come ye to
Bethlehem
Come and behold Him
Born the King of Angels

O come, let us adore Him
O come, let us adore
Him
O come, let us adore Him
Christ the Lord!
O Sing, choirs of angels
Sing in exultation
Sing all that hear in
heaven God's holy word
Give to our Father glory
in the Highest

O come, let us adore Him
O come, let us adore Him
O come, let us adore Him
Christ the Lord!
All Hail! Lord, we greet
Thee Born this happy
morning
O Jesus! for evermore be
Thy name adored
Word of the Father, now in
flesh appearing

Angels From The Realms Of Glory

Angels, from the realms of glory
Wing your flight o'er all the
earth
Ye who sang creation's story
Now proclaim Messiah's birth
Come and worship, come and
worship
Worship Christ, the newborn
King
Shepherds, in the fields abiding
Watching o'er your flocks by
night
God with man is now residing
Yonder shines the infant light
Come and worship, come and
worship Worship Christ, the
newborn King

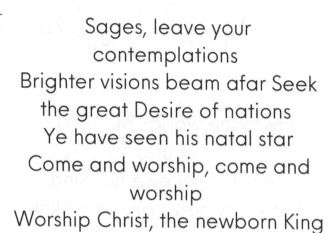

Sages, leave your
contemplations
Brighter visions beam afar Seek
the great Desire of nations
Ye have seen his natal star
Come and worship, come and
worship
Worship Christ, the newborn King

Saints before the altar bending
Watching long in hope and fear
Suddenly the Lord, descending
In his temple shall appear

Come and worship, come and
worship
Worship Christ, the newborn King

Come and worship, come and
worship
Worship Christ, the newborn King

Joy To The World

Joy to the world! The Lord is
come
Let earth receive her King
Let every heart prepare Him
room
And heaven and nature sing
And heaven and nature sing
And heaven, and heaven, and
nature sing

Joy to the Earth! The Saviour
reigns
Let men their songs employ
While fields and floods, rocks,
hills, and plains
Repeat the sounding joy
Repeat the sounding joy
Repeat, repeat the sounding joy

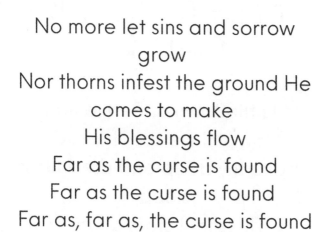

No more let sins and sorrow
grow
Nor thorns infest the ground He
comes to make
His blessings flow
Far as the curse is found
Far as the curse is found
Far as, far as, the curse is found

He rules the world with truth and
grace
And makes the nations prove
The glories of
His righteousness
And wonders of His love
And wonders of
His love And wonders, wonders,
of
His love!

O Little Town Of Bethlehem

O little town of Bethlehem
How still we see thee lie
Above thy deep and dreamless
sleep
The silent stars go by
Yet in thy dark streets shineth The
everlasting light
The hopes and fears of all the
years
Are met in thee tonight
O morning stars, together
Proclaim the holy birth
And praises sing to God the King
And peace to men on earth For
Christ is born of Mary
And gathered all above
While mortals sleep the angels keep
Their watch of wondering love
How silently, how silently

The wondrous gift is given
So God imparts to human hearts
The blessings of His Heaven
No ear may hear His coming
But in this world of sin
Where meek souls will receive Him
still The dear Christ enters in

Where children pure and happy
Pray to the blessed Child
Where Misery cries out to Thee
Son of the Mother mild Where
Charity stands watching
And faith holds wide the door The
dark night wakes, the glory breaks
And Christmas comes once more

O holy Child of Bethlehem
Descend to us we pray Cast out
our sin and enter in Be born in us
today We hear the Christmas
angels The great glad tidings tell
O, come to us, abide with us Our
Lord Emmanuel!

The Virgin Mary Had A Baby Boy

The Virgin Mary had a baby boy
The Virgin Mary had a baby boy
The Virgin Mary had a baby boy
And they say that His name was
Jesus
He come from the glory
He come from the glorious
kingdom He come from the glory
He come from the glorious
kingdom Oh yes, believer! Oh
yes, believer! He come from the
glory
He come from the glorious
kingdom

The angels sang when the baby
born

The angels sang when the baby
born
The angels sang when the baby
born And proclaimed Him the
Saviour Jesus

He come from the glory
He come from the glorious
kingdom He come from the glory
He come from the glorious
kingdom
Oh yes, believer! Oh yes,
believer!
He come from the glory
He come from the glorious
kingdom

The shepherds came where the
baby born
The shepherds came where the
baby born

The shepherds came where the
baby born
And they say that His name was
Jesus

He come from the glory
He come from the glorious
kingdom
He come from the glory
He come from the glorious
kingdom

Oh yes, believer! Oh yes, believer!
He come from the glory
He come from the glorious
kingdom

The Wise Men saw where the
baby born,
The Wise Men saw where the
baby born,

The Wise Men saw where the
baby born,
And they say that His name was
Jesus.

He come from the glory
He come from the glorious
kingdom
He come from the glory
He come from the glorious
kingdom
Oh yes, believer! Oh yes, believer!
He come from the glory
He come from the glorious
kingdom

We Three Kings

We three kings of Orient are
Bearing gifts we traverse afar
Field and fountain, moor and
mountain
Following yonder star

O Star of wonder, star of night
Star with royal beauty bright
Westward leading, still
proceeding
Guide us to thy perfect light

Born a King on Bethlehem's
plain Gold I bring to crown Him
again King forever, ceasing
never
Over us all to reign.

O Star of wonder, star of
night Star with royal beauty
bright

Westward leading, still
proceeding Guide us to thy
perfect light
Frankincense to offer have I
Incense owns a Deity nigh
Prayer and praising, voices
raising Worship Him, God
most high

O Star of wonder, star of
night Star with royal beauty
bright Westward leading, still
proceeding Guide us to thy
perfect light

Myrrh is mine, its bitter
perfume Breathes a life of
gathering gloom

Sorrowing, sighing,
bleeding, dying
Sealed in the stone-cold
tomb

O Star of wonder, star of
night Star with royal beauty
bright Westward leading,
still proceeding
Guide us to thy perfect light

Glorious now behold Him
arise King and God and
sacrifice Heaven sings,
'Alleluia!' 'Alleluia!' the Earth
replies

O Star of wonder, star of
night Star with royal beauty
bright Westward leading,
still proceeding
Guide us to thy perfect light

We Three Kings

O Christmas Tree

O Christmas tree, O
Christmas tree
You stand in splendid
beauty
O Christmas tree, O
Christmas tree
You stand in splendid
beauty

Your branches green in
summer's glow
And evergreen in winter's
snow O Christmas tree, O
Christmas tree
You stand in splendid
beauty

O Christmas tree, O
Christmas tree
You stand in splendid
beauty
O Christmas tree, O
Christmas tree
You stand in splendid
beauty

Your branches green in
summer's glow
And evergreen in winter's
snow
O Christmas tree, O
Christmas tree
You stand in splendid
beauty

Jingle Bells Original

Dashing through the snow
In a one-horse open sleigh
O'er the fields we go Laughing
all the way
Bells on bob tail ring
Making spirits bright
What fun it is to ride and sing
A sleighing song tonight!

Jingle bells, jingle bells Jingle
all the way Oh, what fun it is to
ride
In a one-horse open sleigh,
hey!
Jingle bells, jingle bells
Jingle all the way
Oh, what fun it is to ride
In a one-horse open sleigh!

A day or two ago,
I thought I'd take a ride
And soon, Miss Fanny Bright
Was seated by my side
The horse was lean and lank
Misfortune seemed his lot
He got into a drifted bank
And then we got upsot

Jingle bells, jingle bells Jingle
all the way
Oh, what fun it is to ride In a
one-horse open sleigh, hey!
Jingle bells, jingle bells
Jingle all the way
Oh, what fun it is to ride In a
one-horse open sleigh!

A day or two ago
The story I must tell I went out
on the snow
And on my back I fell

A gent was riding by
In a one-horse open sleigh
He laughed as there I
sprawling lie
But quickly drove away

Jingle bells, jingle bells
Jingle all the way
Oh, what fun it is to ride In a
one-horse open sleigh, hey!
Jingle bells, jingle bells
Jingle all the way
Oh, what fun it is to ride
In a one-horse open sleigh!

Now the ground is white
Go it while you're young
Take the girls tonight
And sing this sleighing song
Just get a bobtailed bay
Two forty as his speed Hitch
him to an open sleigh

And crack! You'll take the lead

Jingle bells, jingle bells
Jingle all the way
Oh, what fun it is to ride In a
one-horse open sleigh, hey!
Jingle bells, jingle bells
Jingle all the way
Oh, what fun it is to ride In a
one-horse open sleigh!

We Wish You A Merry Christmas

We wish you a Merry Christmas
We wish you a Merry Christmas
We wish you a Merry Christmas
And a Happy New Year!

Good tidings we bring to you and your
kin. We wish you a merry Christmas
And a Happy New Year!

Oh, bring us some figgy pudding
Oh, bring us some figgy pudding
Oh, bring us some figgy pudding
And bring it right here!

Good tidings we bring to you and your
kin.
We wish you a merry Christmas
And a Happy New Year!
We won't go until we get some
We won't go until we get some

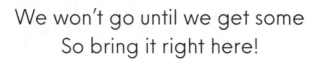

We won't go until we get some
So bring it right here!

Good tidings we bring to you and your
kin.
We wish you a merry Christmas
And a Happy New Year!

We all like our figgy pudding
We all like our figgy pudding
We all like our figgy pudding
With all its good cheer!

Good tidings we bring to you and your
kin
We wish you a merry Christmas
And a Happy New Year!

We wish you a Merry Christmas
We wish you a Merry Christmas
We wish you a Merry Christmas
And a Happy New Year!

This Little Light Of Mine

This little light of mine, I'm gonna let it shine.
This little light of mine, I'm gonna let it shine.
This little light of mine, I'm gonna let it shine.
Let it shine, let it shine, let it shine.

Everywhere I go, I'm gonna let it shine.
Everywhere I go, I'm gonna let it shine.
Everywhere I go, I'm gonna let it shine.
Let it shine, let it shine, let it shine.

This little light of mine, I'm gonna let it shine.
This little light of mine, I'm gonna let it shine.
This little light of mine, I'm gonna let it shine.
Let it shine, let it shine, let it shine.

We will sing in peace, We will sing in harmony.
We will sing in peace, We will sing in harmony.
We will sing in peace, We will sing in harmony.
We will sing in peace, We will sing in harmony.

This little light of mine, I'm gonna let it shine.This little light of mine, I'm gonna let it shine.This little light of mine, I'm gonna let it shine.
Let it shine, let it shine, let it shine.

Let it shine around the world, We're gonna let it shine.
Let it shine around the world, We're gonna let it shine.
Let it shine around the world!
Let it shine, We'll all shine, We'll all shine, We'll all shine! Let shine, let it shine, let it shine!

Away In A Manger

Away in a manger, no
crib for a bed

The little Lord Jesus laid
down His sweet head

The stars in the bright sky
looked down where He
lay

The little Lord Jesus
asleep on the hay

The cattle are lowing, the
baby awakes

But little Lord Jesus, no
crying He makes

I love Thee, Lord Jesus,
look down from the sky

And stay by my cradle till
morning is nigh

Be near me, Lord Jesus, I
ask Thee to stay

Close by me forever, and
love me, I pray

Bless all the dear
children in Thy tender
care

And take us to heaven to
live with Thee there

Ding Dong Merrily On High

Ding dong! Merrily on high

In heav'n the bells are
ringing

Ding dong! Verily the sky
Is riv'n with angel singing

Gloria
Hosanna in excelsis!

E'en so here below, below

Let steeple bells be
swungen
And io, io, io!
By priest and people
sungen

Gloria

Hosanna in excelsis!

Pray you, dutifully prime

Your matin chime, ye
ringers
May you beautifully rime

Your evetime song, ye
singers
Gloria
Hosanna in excelsis!

The First Noel

The first Noel the angels did
say
Was to certain poor
shepherds in fields as they
lay
In fields where they lay
keeping their sheep
On a cold winter's night that
was so deep

Noel, Noel, Noel, Noel Born
is the King of Israel

They looked up and saw a
star Shining in the east,
beyond them far
And to the earth it gave
great light
And so it continued both day
and night

Noel, Noel, Noel, Noel Born
is the King of Israel

And by the light of that same
star Three Wise Men came
from country far
To seek for a King was their
intent
And to follow the star
wherever it went

Noel, Noel, Noel, Noel Born
is the King of Israel

This star drew nigh to the
north-west
O'er Bethlehem it took its
rest
And there it did both stop
and stay
Right over the place where
Jesus lay

Noel, Noel, Noel, Noel
Born is the King of Israel

Then entered in those Wise
Men three
Fell reverently upon their
knee
And offered there in his
presence
Their gold and myrrh and
frankincense

Noel, Noel, Noel, Noel Born
is the King of Israel

Then let us all with one
accord
Sing praises to our heavenly
Lord
That hath made heaven and
earth of naught

And with his blood mankind
hath bought

Noel, Noel, Noel, Noel

Born is the King of Israel

Deck The Halls

Deck the halls with boughs of holly
Fa-la-la-la-la, la-la, la, la
'Tis the season to be jolly Fa-la-la-la-la, la-la, la, la

Don we now our gay apparel
Fa-la-la, la-la-la, la, la, la
Troll the ancient Yule-tide carol Fa-la-la-la-la, la-la, la, la

See the blazing Yule before us
Fa-la-la-la-la, la-la, la, la
Strike the harp and join the chorus Fa-la-la-la-la, la-la, la, la

Follow me in merry measure
Fa-la-la-la-la, la-la, la, la
While I tell of Yuletide
treasure Fa-la-la-la-la, la-
la, la, la

Fast away the old year
passes
Fa-la-la-la-la, la-la, la, la
Hail the new, ye lads and
lasses Fa-la-la-la-la, la-la,
la, la

Sing we joyous all together
Fa-la-la-la-la, la-la, la, la
Heedless of the wind and
weather
Fa-la-la-la-la, la-la, la, la
Fa-la-la-la-la, la-la, la, la

Silent Night

Silent night, holy night
All is calm, all is bright
Round yon Virgin Mother and
Child
Holy infant so tender and
mild
Sleep in heavenly peace
Sleep in heavenly peace

Silent night, holy night
Shepherds quake at the sight
Glories stream from heaven
afar
Heavenly hosts sing Alleluia
Christ, the Saviour is born
Christ, the Saviour is born

Silent night, holy night Son of
God, love's pure light

Radiant beams from Thy holy
face
With the dawn of redeeming
grace
Jesus, Lord, at Thy birth
Jesus, Lord, at Thy birth

Silent night, holy night
All is calm, all is bright
Round yon Virgin Mother and
Child
Holy infant so tender and
mild
Sleep in heavenly peace
Sleep in heavenly peace

Go Tell It On The Mountain

Go tell it on the mountain
Over the hills and everywhere
Go tell it on the mountain
That Jesus Christ is born!

While shepherds kept their
watching
O'er silent flocks by night
Behold throughout the heavens
There shone a holy light

Go tell it on the mountain
Over the hills and everywhere
Go tell it on the mountain That
Jesus Christ is born!

The shepherds feared and
trembled
When lo above the earth Rang
out the angel chorus

That hailed our Saviour's birth

And I said go!
Go tell it on the mountain
Over the hills and everywhere
Go tell it on the mountain
That Jesus Christ is born!

Down in a lowly manger
Our humble Christ was born
And God sent us salvation
That blessed this Christmas morn

And I said go! Go tell it on the
mountain
Over the hills and everywhere
Go tell it on the mountain
That Jesus Christ is born!

Go tell it on the mountain Over
the hills and everywhere Go tell
it on the mountain That Jesus
Christ is born! That Jesus Christ is
born!

Auld Lang Syne

Happy New Year!
Should old acquaintance be
forgot
And never brought to mind?
Should old acquaintance be
forgot
In the days of auld lang syne?

For auld lang syne, my dear
For auld lang syne
We'll take a cup of kindness yet
For the sake of auld lang syne

And surely you'll buy your pint
cup!
And surely I'll buy mine!
And we'll take a cup o' kindness
yet For the sake of auld lang
syne
For auld lang syne, my dear

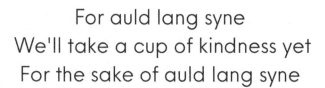

For auld lang syne
We'll take a cup of kindness yet
For the sake of auld lang syne

We two have run about the
slopes
And picked the daisies fine
We've wandered many a weary
foot
Since the days of auld lang syne

For auld lang syne, my dear
For auld lang syne
We'll take a cup of kindness yet
For the sake of auld lang syne

We two have paddled in the
stream
From morning sun till dine
But seas between us broad have
roared
Since the days of auld lang syne

For auld lang syne, my dear for
auld lang syne
we'll take a cup of kindness yet
for the sake of auld lang syne

And there's a hand my trusty
friend!
And give me a hand o' thine!
We'll take a cup of kindness yet
for the days of auld lang syne

For auld lang syne, my dear for
auld lang syne
we'll take a cup of kindness yet
for the sake of auld lang syne

For auld lang syne, my dear
for auld lang syne
we'll take a cup of kindness yet
for the sake of auld lang syne

Auld Lang Syne

The Christmas Song

Chestnuts roasting on an open fire
Jack Frost nipping at your nose
Yuletide carols being sung by a
choir
And folks dressed up like Eskimos

Everybody knows a turkey and some
Mistletoe help to make the season
bright
Tiny tots with their eyes all aglow
Will find it hard to sleep tonight

They know that Santa's on his way
He's loaded lots of toys and goodies
On his sleigh
And every mother's
Child is gonna spy to see if
Reindeer really know how to fly

And so, I'm offering this
Simple phrase to kids from
One to ninety-two
Altho' it's been said many times
Many ways
"Merry Christmas to you"

Coventry Carol

Lully, lullay, thou little tiny
child,
Bye bye, lully, lullay.
Lully, lullay, thou little tiny
child,
Bye bye, lully, lullay.

O sisters too, how may we
do
For to preserve this day
This poor youngling for whom
we sing,
"Bye bye, lully, lullay"?

Herod the king, in his raging,
Charged he hath this day
His men of might in his own
sight
All young children to slay.

That woe is me, poor child, for thee
And ever mourn and may
For thy parting neither say nor sing,
"Bye bye, lully, lullay."

Do You Hear What I Hear?

Said the night wind to the little
lamb,
do you see what I see
Way up in the sky, little lamb,
do you see what I see
A star, a star, dancing in the night
With a tail as big as a kite
With a tail as big as a kite

Said the little lamb to the
shepherd boy,
do you hear what I hear
Ringing through the sky, shepherd
boy,
do you hear what I hear
A song, a song, high above the
trees
With a voice as big as the sea
With a voice as big as the sea

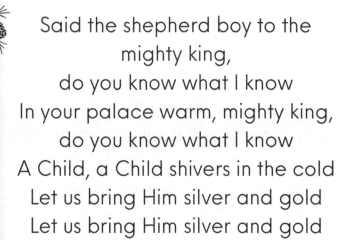

Said the shepherd boy to the
mighty king,
do you know what I know
In your palace warm, mighty king,
do you know what I know
A Child, a Child shivers in the cold
Let us bring Him silver and gold
Let us bring Him silver and gold

Said the king to the people
everywhere,
listen to what I say
Pray for peace, people
everywhere!
listen to what I say
The Child, the Child, sleeping in
the night
He will bring us goodness and
light
He will bring us goodness and
light

Frosty the Snowman

Frosty the Snowman, was a jolly
happy soul,
With a corn cob pipe and a button
nose, and two eyes made of coal.
Frosty the Snowman, is a fairytale,
they say.
He was made of snow, but the
children know he came to life one
day.
There must have been some magic in
that old silk hat they found,
For when they placed it on his head,
he began to dance around!
Oh, Frosty, the Snowman, was alive
as he could be;
and the children say he could laugh
and play,
just the same as you and me.
Thumpety thump, thump, thumpety
thump, thump,
look at Frosty go.

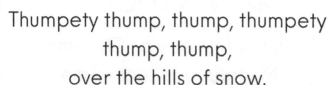

Thumpety thump, thump, thumpety
thump, thump,
over the hills of snow.
Frosty the Snowman, knew the sun was
hot that day,
so he said, "Let's run, and we'll have
some fun now, before I melt away."
Down to the village, with a broomstick
in his hand,
Running here and there, all around the
square,
sayin', "Catch me if you can."
He led them down the streets of town,
right to the traffic cop;
and only paused a moment, when he
heard him holler, "Stop!"
For Frosty, the Snowman, had to hurry
on his way,
But he waved goodbye, sayin' "Don't
cry, I'll be back again some day."

12 Days Of Christmas

On the first day of Christmas
My true love sent to me
A partridge in a pear tree

On the second day of Christmas
My true love sent to me Two
turtle doves and
A partridge in a pear tree

On the third day of Christmas
My true love sent to me
Three French hens
Two turtle doves and
A partridge in a pear tree

On the forth day of Christmas
My true love sent to me
Four calling birds Three French
hens
Two turtle doves and

A partridge in a pear tree

On the fifth day of Christmas
My true love sent to me
Five golden rings
Four calling birds
Three French hens
Two turtle doves and
A partridge in a pear tree

On the sixth day of Christmas
My true love sent to me
Six geese a-laying
Five golden rings
Four calling birds
Three French hens
Two turtle doves and
A partridge in a pear tree

On the seventh day of Christmas
My true love sent to me
Seven swans a-swimming
Six geese a-laying

Five golden rings
Four calling birds
Three French hens
Two turtle doves and
A partridge in a pear tree

On the eighth day of Christmas
My true love sent to me
Eight maids a-milking
Seven swans a-swimming
Six geese a-laying
Five golden rings Four calling
birds
Three French hens Two turtle
doves and
A partridge in a pear tree

On the ninth day of Christmas
My true love sent to me
Nine ladies dancing
Eight maids a-milking
Seven swans a-swimming
Six geese a-laying

Five golden rings
Four calling birds
Three French hens
Two turtle doves and
A partridge in a pear tree

On the tenth day of Christmas
My true love sent to me
Ten lords a-leaping
Nine ladies dancing
Eight maids a-milking
Seven swans a-swimming
Six geese a-laying
Five golden rings
Four calling birds
Three French hens
Two turtle doves and
A partridge in a pear tree

On the eleventh day of Christmas
My true love sent to me
Eleven pipers piping
Ten lords a-leaping

Nine ladies dancing
Eight maids a-milking
Seven swans a-swimming
Six geese a-laying
Five golden rings
Four calling birds
Three French hens
Two turtle doves and
A partridge in a pear tree

Eight maids a-milking
Seven swans a-swimming
Six geese a-laying
Five golden rings
Four calling birds
Three French hens
Two turtle doves and
A partridge in a pear tree

12

Day Of Chrismas

Carols are The Soul
of Christmas

13406153R00042